Teddy Bears

Match the numeral on the clothespin to the numeral on the teddy bear.

Materials:

- Ten wood clasp clothespins; permanent marking pen

Directions:

- With permanent marker, write a numeral from one to ten on the end of each clothespin.

Extension:

- Have the children bring in a teddy bear or other stuffed animal. Group the toys in sets of one to ten. Direct the children to match the clothespin to the set.

Ants

Student Directions:

> Match the numeral on the clothespin to the same number of ants.

Materials:

- Ten wood clasp clothespins; permanent marking pen

Directions:

- With permanent marker, write a numeral from one to ten on the end of each clothespin.

Extensions:

- Pack a picnic basket with plastic utensils. Have students make sets of 1-10.
- Obtain plastic ants (available at party supply and toy stores). Direct students to make sets of 1-10 and match them to the sets on the gameboard.

Trucks

Student Directions:

> Find the missing numerals. Attach clothespins so the numbers are in order.

Materials:

- Five wood clasp clothespins; permanent marking pen

Directions:

- With permanent marker, write a numeral (2, 3, 5, 8, 10) on the end of the clothespin.

Extension:

- Write the numerals one to ten in order.

Monkey

> Match the number to the number name.

Materials:

- Ten wood clasp clothespins; permanent marking pen

Directions:

- With permanent marker, write a numeral from one to ten on the end of each clothespin.

Extensions:

- Recite the rhyme ''Ten Little Monkeys!''
- Tell students to jump like monkeys. Call out the number of times you want them to jump.
- To reinforce number names, have students bring in old T-shirts. Paint number names on the front and matching numbers on the back.

Penguin Finger Poke

Preparation:

- You will need a one-hole punch, craft sticks, stapler, and a marking pen.

- Cut out the penguin shape (optional); punch out the indicated holes.

- Turn the penguin over and write the number that comes next by the corresponding hole.

- Staple two craft sticks together to the bottom of the penguin, placing one stick on each side of the penguin.

To play:

- One child faces the front of the penguin while the teacher (or another child) faces the back of the penguin.

- The child facing the front of the penguin puts his index finger through any hole and says aloud the number that comes next.

- The teacher (or child) facing the back, checks the answer.

- If two children are playing, they exchange places when all numbers are read.

Frog Finger Poke

Preparation:

- You will need scissors, a one-hole punch, craft sticks, stapler, and a marking pen.

- Cut out the frog shape (optional); punch out the indicated holes.

- Turn the frog over and write the number of the set next to the corresponding hole.

- Staple two craft sticks together to the bottom of the frog, placing one stick on each side of the frog.

To play:

- One child faces the front of the frog while the teacher (or another child) faces the back of the frog.

- The child facing the front of the frog puts his index finger through any hole and says aloud the number of the set.

- The teacher (or child) facing the back, checks the answer.

- If two children are playing, they exchange places when all numbers have been read.

Forest Gameboard

Materials:

- Game cards; 20 markers (beans, coins, buttons, etc.)

Directions:

- Two or three may play this game.

- Place game cards in a pile on the tree.

- Determine which player goes first.

- The first player draws a card from the pile.

- Match the set on the card to the number on the gameboard. Place a marker on that space. Play until all spaces have been covered.

Extensions:

- Make two sets of game pieces labeled with number names. Play the game using the number names instead of the number set game cards.

- Using sticky dots, cover sides of a die and label with 1's and 2's or use a spinner with 1's and 2's. Have children take turns rolling the die and moving the indicated number of spaces. Have them say the number that is on that space.

Note: Be sure to make a copy of the directions above if you use the gameboard as a file folder game. Glue the directions to the front of the file folder.

Forest Game Cards

Directions:

Cut apart on the solid lines. Mix up the cards and place on the gameboard.

Jack-in-the-Box

Student Directions:

> Lace the Jack-in-the-Box starting at one and ending at ten.

Materials:

- One-hole punch; approximately one yard (one meter) of yarn or a shoe lace; glue or tape

Directions:

- Punch out the indicated holes on the Jack-in-the-Box.

- Tape or glue (allow to dry before using) one end of the yarn and tie a knot in the other end.

- Instruct the child to use the taped end of the yarn to begin lacing.

Extensions:

- Make word number cards. Have students match them to the words on the Jack-in-the-Box.

- Direct students to lace the card in reverse order beginning with the number word ten.

two

one

three

four

ten

five

nine

six

eight

seven

MOON WHEEL

Directions:

- Cut out the wheel and the spaces marked "Cut out."

- Attach the number words wheel (on the next page) behind the moon with a paper fastener through the center.

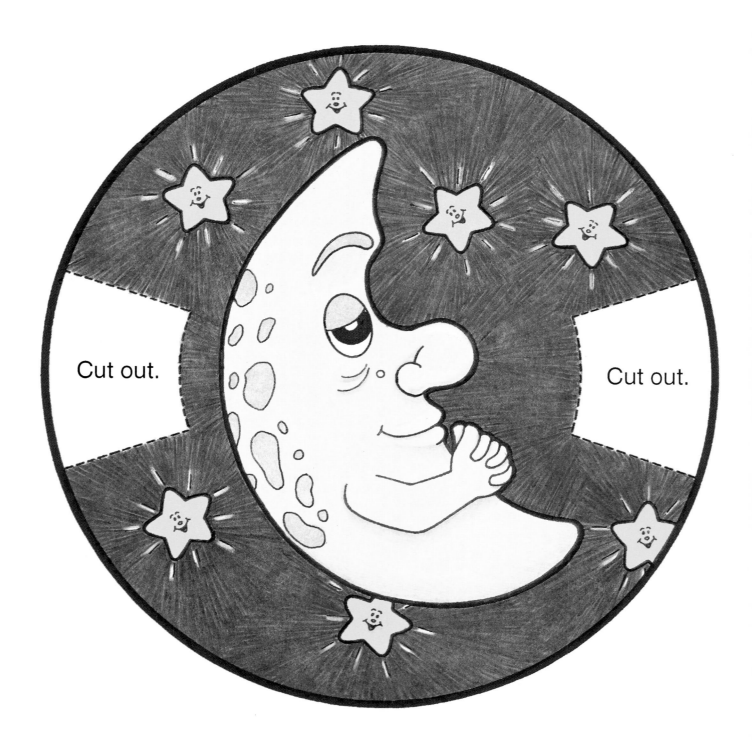

Moon

Directions:

- Cut out the number words wheel and attach behind the moon as directed.

- Have the child hold the bottom circle in one hand and rotate the top circle with the other hand.

- As the child moves the wheel, direct him to focus on each number name set and numeral.

Extensions:

- Use blocks, counters, buttons, or other objects to make sets for each number.

- Make a set of number word cards. Tell the students to match them to the numbers 1 to 5 on a clock face.

MOON WHEEL *(Cont.)*

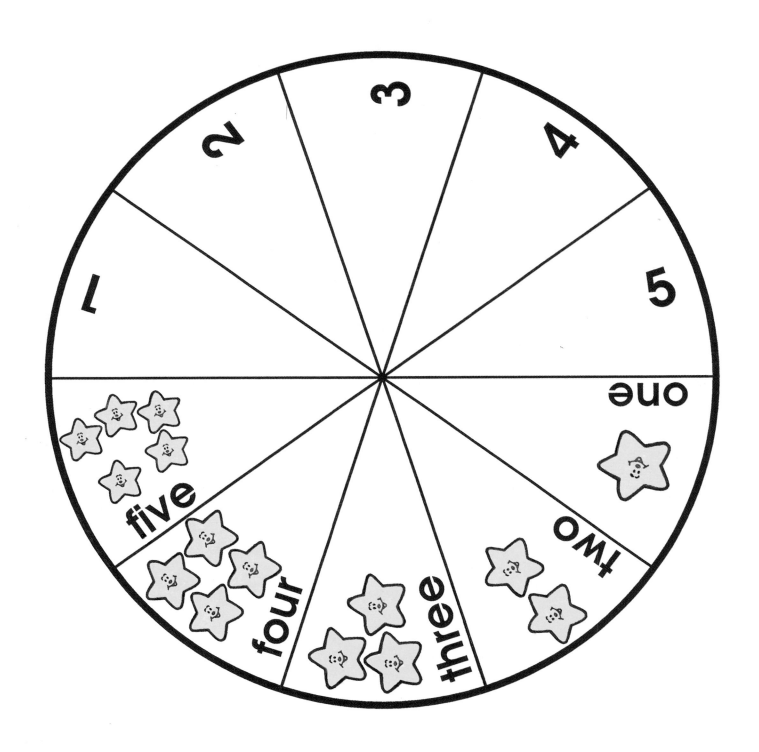

Directions:

- Cut out the wheel and the spaces marked ''Cut out.''
- Attach the number words wheel (on the next page) behind the sun with a paper fastener through the center.

Sun

Directions:

- Cut out the number words wheel and attach behind the sun as directed.

- Have the child hold the bottom circle in one hand and rotate the top circle with the other hand.

- As the child moves the wheel, direct him to focus on each number name set and numeral.

Extensions:

- Direct the child to stop the wheel. Have him tell you which number comes before or after.

- Make a set of number word cards. Tell the students to match them to the numbers 6 to 10 on a clock face.

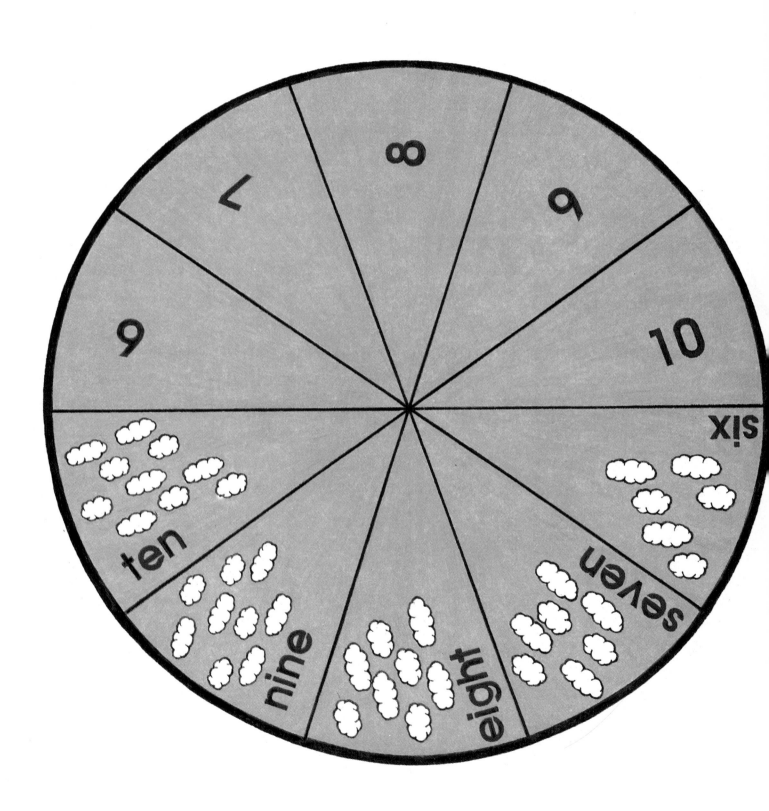